THE JANUARY 6 COMMITTEE REPORT IN A NUTSHELL

THE JANUARY 6 COMMITTEE REPORT IN A NUTSHELL

with Study Questions

WILLIAM R LONG
M DIV, PH D, J D

ISBN: 978-1-7350927-5-1

Book Design by Sarah Katreen Hoggatt
Printed in the United States of America

Contents

Preface

I WROTE THIS BOOK TO TRY TO understand what the January 6 Select Committee ("Committee") presented in its Report of the events in Washington DC before and during the occupation of the US Capitol on January 6, 2021. I wrote it not with a desire to attack or impugn the motives of the Committee nor to cheer them on in their task, but simply to understand what they wrote.

As I began my task I soon realized that what the Committee presents to us, in 814 pages, is far too long for almost anyone to sit down and read. Even the Executive Summary, at 193 pages, is much too imposing. We needed something longer than a news story or a magazine article but shorter than the Executive Summary that gets at the heart of the report.

This short book is an attempt to fill that need. Each chapter is no more than five pages in length, and the entire book can be read in one sitting. Look at each chapter as a kind of snack or appetizer, one that could become a full meal but often is a teaser to whet one's appetite to taste or learn more. As a result of reading a chapter, some may want to examine that topic in more detail, and I show you ways you can do that.

My hope is that this book will aid in disseminating knowledge not just of the events of January 6, 2021 in our Nation's Capital, but of the series of events between the Presidential election on November 3, 2020 and the final Congressional certification of Joe Biden's victory in the wee hours of January 7, 2021.

As mentioned, the tone I try to strike in this book is reportorial and respectful. I respect the work of the Committee as well as you, my reader. You will come to your own conclusions about that day and its meaning for your life or in the life of our Nation, and I hope to be able here to make accessible some very important material to help you move toward your conclusion.

Two brief comments on my own perspective. First, I do believe in the idea and promise of America and that America, despite massive flaws, is a good place and one that needs to be cared for and preserved. This book is my small attempt to show that "care." Then, even though I wrestle with how to describe the events of January 6, 2021 at the Capitol (see Chapter Thirteen), I believe the illegal occupation of the Capitol was a bad thing for our country and that those involved in the illegal activities should be held accountable.

How This Book is Organized

In addition to this Preface, this book consists of thirteen chapters and an Appendix. The first chapter gives an overview of the Committee Report, focusing on the seven themes that are most important to the Committee. Chapters two and three present the leading findings of the Executive Summary (pp. 1-193). Usually the Executive Summary of a report is a brief and faithfully abbreviated version of a longer report, but in this case the Executive Summary is very long and launches into areas not covered directly by the Report. I try to highlight the flow of the Executive Summary, though it is impossible to cover every issue it mentions.

Then, chapters four through eleven include one chapter each on one of the seven themes as well as one separate chapter the Report calls "Analysis of the Attack." The goal is to give you a sense of both the complexities as well as what is at stake with each of the Committee's chapters of the Report. I try to vary my focus, because the Report covers so much, and therefore sometimes my focus is on chronology, such as tracing important events that happened in the nearly 3 ½ hours of occupation of the Capitol by protesters on January 6 but sometimes my focus is simply explaining an issue, such as Vice-President Pence's role on January 6, 2021.

Chapter twelve discusses the Appendices to the Report. Especially important in these Appendices is the discussion of the role of the police and military establishment on January 6. Chapter thirteen asks a question that the Committee never discussed—how we actually should refer to the events of January 6, 2021. I believe it is important that we think about words and their implications in this chapter, and I invite you to join me in that task. Finally, my Appendix briefly presents the criminal charges that the Committee believes could appropriately be brought by the Special Prosecutor assigned to the case as well as several topics the Committee felt they couldn't explore in detail.

Suggestions for Using this Book

I wrote this book with four audiences in mind. Three of them are groups and the fourth is individual study. The groups include, first, high school civics or social studies classes, where a unit on the events between November 3, 2020 and January 6, 2021, would be particularly timely. To aid that effort, I have ended each chapter with a brief set of questions designed to aid group discussion.

I also aim this book this at classes of college students and have thus added a few research-oriented questions at the end of each chapter to stimulate further understanding. Therefore each chapter has two types of questions at the end: questions for clarification of ideas and discussion and questions for further study and research. My hope, also, is that there may be book clubs or citizen clubs that might find this nutshell useful. Finally, I urge individuals to use this book to launch their own investigation into the events between November 3, 2020 and January 6, 2021.

Each chapter can be read in about 5-10 minutes, but the questions at the end of each chapter are designed to encourage pursuit of additional areas of interest that might lead in some instances to formulating one's own test questions, research projects, or further topics to understand. I have also at times tried to help you, the reader, imagine yourself in a position that you most likely *didn't occupy*, such as that of a peaceful protester at the Capitol or a federal police officer on January 6, and wonder what you would have felt or done.

My own recommendation is that the following chapters would provide the most useful study and discussion opportunities:

- Chapter One: The Introduction, Seven Themes and one "Analysis" in the Report
- Chapters Four-Eleven: Each chapter deals with one of the Eight areas mentioned in Chapter One in greater detail
- Chapter Thirteen: How we Should Refer to the Events of January 6, 2021 at the US Capitol

Acknowledgments

THOUGH SEVERAL PEOPLE HAVE ENCOURAGED ME in this project, I want to single out three here who were kind enough to read and offer a critique of this book. The first is Jon Hagmaier, a former student of mine, who has made a career of launching successful start-up companies in the education and board-gaming worlds. John's energy, intellectual savvy, generosity of spirit, and CEO-like ability to see the whole rather than just the details, has made this a better work. Then, the Hon. Henry Breithaupt, a friend of more than a generation, gave timely feedback inspired by his long legal career representing clients and on the bench. Finally, Mr Joel Ario, an accomplished insurance regulator with a rich background in law, theology and the political process, brought his extensive knowledge to each page and each claim I made. Their words, but even more their faithful friendship, means more to me than I can indicate here.

CHAPTER 1

Introduction and Seven Themes

Introduction to the Report

The final version of the long-awaited report of the Select Committee to look into the Attack on the US Capitol on January 6, 2021, in connection with the certification of Joe Biden's win as President of the United States, was published in late December 2022. It appeared a few months after an influential conservative group of eight prominent former judges, attorneys and politicians investigated the more than 60 cases filed in Federal and State courts after the election of 2020 alleging fraud in the Presidential election. The result of their investigation, released in mid-July 2022 and entitled *Lost, Not Stolen*, indicates their conclusion in the title. These conservative Republican jurists and politicians found no credible reason for assertions of massive voter fraud in connection with the 2020 Presidential election.

The conclusion of the January 6 Committee echoes that of the jurists and politicians, even though they had a much broader charge than that group. Their charge was to investigate "the facts, circumstances and causes that led to this attack on the Capitol, the Congress and the Constitution."

So, they collected data, interviewed witnesses, held multiple public hearings, and drafted and revised their the report for seventeen months before releasing their findings. In a word, the report is massive. The Executive Summary, which in many documents is no more than a page or two, runs to more than 190 pages. The text and appendices of the report itself are another 620 pages. The report is copiously annotated. Its basic thesis is clear from the beginning—that the January 6, 2021 Attack on the US Capitol was the culmination of an effort by outgoing President Trump to try to undermine the results of the 2020 Presidential Election by using several strategies.[1] The remainder of this essay will present those strategies, which will then be discussed more fully in chapters 4-11.

Post-Election Strategies of President Trump and His Supporters to Overturn the Election Results

Those strategies, in the order in which they occurred beginning election evening, November 3, 2020, included the following:

First, to proclaim victory in the election on the very night of the election, even before the votes were sufficiently counted in most states. Then when the numbers began favoring Biden in the

---

[1] In her introductory remarks, Liz Cheney mentions the President's seven-part strategy to overturn the election result. The Committee Report, however, is organized around eight chapters, though one could argue that there really are seven themes (chapters 1-7) and one "analysis" (chapter 8) to consider. This book will devote one chapter to each of the Committee's eight chapters. One important additional theme, the filing of 60+ lawsuits in many of the battle-ground states after the election to try to show fraud in the voting in these states, was not treated at all by the Committee. They no doubt felt that the report noted in the text: *Lost, Not Stolen* did a sufficiently thorough job that they didn't need to repeat that work.

next two days, to continue to maintain the claim of victory but to add to this claim, often in the most impassioned language, that the election was "stolen." This was done despite the fact that his closest advisors told the President that it was too early for him to proclaim victory (or concede) on the day of or shortly after the election. Counting of absentee ballots sometimes takes a few days. The Committee presents the testimony or statements of several people who said that the plan falsely to declare victory on election night was part of the President's pre-planned strategy: first you proclaim victory and then, if it doesn't seem to be working out that way, you proclaim "fraud" in the election.

Second—a two-part strategy with state officials. One was to pressure state election officials in seven battleground states, where the legislatures were largely controlled by Republicans but the popular vote went to Biden to "find" additional votes for him. Then, two, to convene groups of sympathetic state legislators to urge them to call Special Sessions in their respective states and, if sufficient evidence in their state of fraud could be asserted or claimed, to take over the electoral function from the people and express the people's will by appointing a pro-Trump slate of electors.

Third, to devise a method by which Republicans in each of the seven battleground states would come up with alternative slates of electors, submit them to the proper officials, and thereby present the problem of competing slates of electors to the Congress when they certified the electoral vote count on January 6, 2021.

Fourth, to replace outgoing Attorney General William Barr with a more junior attorney supportive of President Trump's efforts who would pressure states not to certify results of the election. This would involve the Federal Department of Justice in an effort to write letters to legislators in these seven battleground or swing states saying that the Department of Justice had found sufficient evidence of fraud in their ballots that they ought not to permit the certification of electors.

Fifth, to pressure Vice-President Mike Pence, when the Joint Session of Congress convened for the counting of the electoral votes on January 6, to see his role as not just counting votes but making choices as to the legitimacy of certain slates of electors. This would entail either disallowing the electoral votes in the seven contested states (all of which were won by Biden) thus giving President Trump the victory or, more likely, declaring that the alternative slates of electors submitted meant that the votes had to be returned to the states to reconsider whether fraud had occurred and to certify the "correct" (i.e., Republican) electors.

Sixth—to call thousands of people, some of them armed and dangerous, to Washington DC on January 6, 2021 and to urge them in an hour-long speech on the Ellipse to march to the Capitol to "take back" the country, which led to the events of the afternoon and early evening of January 6, 2021 at the Capitol.

Seventh—to do nothing in a crucial 187 minutes (1:10 p.m. – 4:17 p.m.) on the afternoon of January 6, after a riot was declared at the US Capitol, either to call off the protesters, or to assure that sufficient police and others were in place to contain and reverse the illegal occupation of the US Capitol.

Then there is an eighth chapter, though not an additional theme, that goes through what the Committee calls an "Analysis of the Attack" on the Capitol on January 6, 2021 in a minute-by-minute fashion. One might see this as a mirror image of the Seventh factor—while the President was being derelict in duty, to use the Committee's phrase, the people he called to the Capitol were very actively involved in occupying that space, leading to the postponement of the electoral count. Finally the Capitol was cleared of protesters and order was restored so that Congress could resume its work by mid-evening of January 6 and conclude about 3:30 a.m. on January 7.

Questions for Discussion and Further Investigation

1. Which of the seven post-election strategies of President Trump and his supporters or the "Analysis of the Attack" listed above would you like to study further? Why?
2. Construct a calendar showing the significant events in the process of electing a President in the United States, from election day (early in November) until Inauguration Day on January 20 of the next year.
3. Many people know precisely where they were on important days in our recent national history (the assassination of John Kennedy for older people; the 9/11 terrorist attacks for many younger people). Where were you and what were you doing during the hours of the occupation of the US Capitol on January 6, 2021?
4. Do you know anyone personally who was involved in the events in Washington DC on January 6, 2021?

Chapter 2

Executive Summary: Three Important Themes

THE PURPOSE OF THIS CHAPTER IS twofold: to give you a flavor of the flow of the Executive Summary of the Report and then to explore the first three Findings of Fact that the Committee lays out on page 4.

The first thing to note is that the Executive Summary is l-o-n-g; indeed it is too long to be properly called by that name. If you were to be handed a 200-page report with an Executive Summary, your first thought would be that the Summary should be no more than 2 or 3 pages in length. After all, it is a *summary*. What makes the Executive Summary of this Report off-putting is that, including notes and treatment of topics that the main report doesn't handle, it is 193 pages long. I will attempt in this and the next essay to get at the most important points, but the sheer length will present an obstacle for many readers of the Report.

When the Committee actually turns to its summary, however, it gives priceless information. It has broken its information down

7

into 17 Findings (pp. 4-7). In this essay I cover the first 3 Findings. They are:

Findings 1-2: Beginning election night (November 3) and continuing through January 6, President Trump disseminated false allegations of fraud related to the Presidential election. These allegations were disputed almost unanimously by his senior staff. In addition by mid-December his legal team had lost more than sixty election lawsuits alleging fraud, winning only one minor one, and his senior advisors urged him to admit defeat.

It all began at 2:20 a.m. on Wednesday, November 4, 2020, just hours after the polls had closed on the West coast and before enough votes were counted in many states to declare a winner. The President was up, and he said the following, "This is a fraud on the American public. This is an embarrassment to our country. We were getting ready to win this election. Frankly, we did win this election." Reading between these contradictory lines (why would he claim fraud if he had won?), one sees a two-part election strategy starting to unfold, which the Committee lays out in great detail. This was a strategy actually devised well before the election itself. The first part would be for the President to declare victory late in the evening of Election Day, when the initial results favored Republicans (as is usually the case in National elections). Then the second part would be that as the results of absentee and mail-in ballots were counted, which historically tended to favor Democrats, the President would declare that fraud was at work, that the counting of votes should stop and the Supreme Court should declare him the winner.

Once all the major news outlets called the election for Joe Biden on Saturday November 7, President Trump's claims of fraud only intensified. This was despite the near-unanimous word of senior officials that Joe Biden had won. Attorney General William Barr said, "I repeatedly told the President in no uncertain terms that I did not see evidence of fraud. . .that would have affected the outcome of the election." Mike Pence, the Vice-President, said, "There was never evidence of widespread fraud. . .I told the President that, once the legal challenges played out (by mid-December), he should simply accept the outcome of the election."

Nevertheless, the President forcefully argued that the election was "stolen," and he managed in the process to convince countless followers that this was true. After all, if your President is so vociferous about something about which he is in a unique position to know about, couldn't you understand how many would believe what he said? But the Report points out in agonizing detail how none of the specific allegations of fraud were substantiated either in a court of law or in the admission of officials overseeing elections.

Finding 3: Despite knowing that such an action would be illegal, and that no State submitted more than one slate of electors for the Congressional joint session on January 6, 2021, when the final electoral tally was made, President Trump pressured Vice President Pence to refuse to count electoral votes from seven key battleground states. If Pence had refused to do this, and removed these electoral votes from the official count, the election would have gone to President Trump, by an electoral vote of 232-222.

At issue here in this Finding was the authority and role of the Vice President acting as President of the Senate as the electoral votes were counted on January 6, 2021. The central question, in legal terms, is whether the Vice-President had a substantive or only a ministerial role. What a substantive role means is that he had the authority, on his own, to declare something like the following hypothetical, 'There have been reports of voter irregularity in seven states. Rather than including them, I will remove them from the electoral count, leaving President Trump with a 232-222 victory' (The actual number certified by Congress on January 6 was 306 electoral votes for Biden and 232 for Trump). Or, more likely, if the Vice-President had a substantive role, he

The January 6 Report in a Nutshell

could have said, 'I detect there were voter irregularities in seven states. I hereby refer the issue back to the state legislatures of those states (which were conveniently controlled by Republicans in six of them and tied in the seventh) for them to investigate claims of fraud and return with a corrected slate of electors.'

The reasoning behind these two hypothetical statements was provided by Prof John Eastman, who argued in a series of memos that the Vice-President had substantive power to do this. Everyone else who had studied the issue had concluded that the Twelfth Amendment to the Constitution, as well as the Electoral Count Act of 1887 only gave the Vice-President a ministerial role—to announce the results of the electoral votes submitted by the states. All others than Eastman had argued that it would have been ludicrous for the Founding Fathers, who were breaking away from English tyranny and one person royal rule, to have vested the power to declare victory of the Presidential election in one person. On January 6, Vice-President Pence decided he had no power to do what Professor Eastman argued and President Trump was pressuring him to do. And, as the Committee Report lays out in the following chapters, he could have paid for this loyalty to the Constitution with his life.

Questions for Discussion and Further Investigation

1. When would you say is the proper time to concede defeat in a Presidential election? When the news networks call the election? When your senior advisors tell you it's over? On December 14 after the electors meet in all the states and cast their electoral votes? Only when you become personally satisfied that all of your objections are sufficiently answered? Never, if you believe you are right?
2. Explain the difference between a substantive and ministerial role for the Vice President during the counting of electoral votes on January 6 after a Presidential Election.

3. Professor John Eastman developed crucially important theories of the powers of the Vice-President in certifying the electoral vote on January 6.What can you learn about his memos and his theories?

4. Section 15 of the Electoral Count Act of 1887 details the duties of the Vice President on the day of counting of electoral votes. Find that section of law, read what it says and discuss whether you think the law is clear on that issue.

CHAPTER 3

The Remainder of Executive Summary

THE REST OF THE EXECUTIVE SUMMARY, especially Findings 4-15, covers several topics that can conveniently be grouped in three categories:

- First—attempts to pressure state election officials and Republican state legislators to submit alternative slates of electors in several key battleground states;
- Second—a plan to replace outgoing Attorney General William Barr with a pro-Trump junior attorney who would use the resources of the Federal Department of Justice to say that the election was tainted with fraud;
- Third—multiple efforts to call radical groups to Washington DC on January 6, 2021 to try to stop the Congress from certifying the electoral victory of Joe Biden as President.

The Appendix to this book will deal with the subject of the criminal charges the Committee recommends (on pp. 103-113 of the Report) be brought against Donald Trump for his efforts to overturn the election results as well as a few topics the Committee didn't address. Let's turn now to each of these three issues listed above.

Pressure on State Officials and the Fake Elector Strategy

December 14, 2020 was so crucial in electing the President because on that date the electors of the Presidential candidate who garnered the most popular votes in each state met in their respective state Capitols to cast their electoral votes for the victorious candidate. Each elector of the victorious candidate would sign an electoral vote certificate. Then a Certificate of Ascertainment, signed by the Governor with the state seal affixed, declaring how many votes each Presidential candidate received, would be sent to several places, among them the National Archives in Washington DC and the federal House and Senate. The electors who cast their votes in this manner were the official electors of the state.

What happened in at seven states (AZ, GA, MI, NM, NV, PA, WI) was that alternative slates of electors, which the Committee calls "fake electors," were created. Each of these states had been called for Joe Biden when all the major networks announced Biden's victory on November 7. These alternative or "fake" slates, prepared by Republicans in these seven states, mimicked the official slates but didn't have the state seal or Governor's signature, but they were also sent to the appropriate Washington DC officials. The plan was to create confusion on January 6 so that Vice-President Pence would be confronted with two contrary slates of electors. both claiming legitimacy, from several states. The hope of those devising the "fake elector" strategy was that Pence would stop the electoral count and either remove that state from the electoral vote or send the entire issue of the proper electoral slate back to these state legislature (all controlled by Republicans except PA, which was equally divided).

In addition, in several of these battleground states, pressure was exerted on election officials to "find" additional votes for the President or to declare that the there was enough fraud or uncertainty in the election results that the final tally was tainted. The hope was that the state legislature, then, would see it as their task to meet and name the right (i.e., Republican) slate of electors.

Pressure on the Federal Department of Justice

President Trump's hand-picked Attorney General William Barr began to cause problems for him after election day. As early as November 23 he told the President that the Department of Justice was investigating every fraud allegation regarding the election, but that none of the allegations was "meritorious." Then, on December 1, Barr told the Associated Press that the Department had not seen fraud on a scale that would have led to a different outcome. Shortly thereafter, Barr announced he would rather summarily leave his post.

The three weeks between Barr's departure in mid-December 2020 and the Congressional joint session on January 6 were a flurry of activity, as the President directly, and through his senior staff, orchestrated a campaign to have the Department of Justice send a letter to state legislatures announcing that there was significant fraud in the Presidential election and that the states needed to look into it. This proposal sent shock waves through the Department because it was evident that this was an attempt to co-opt the Department for the President's political agenda. Finally, when the President wanted to appoint a junior attorney (Clark) to become Acting Attorney General, and send out the letter just mentioned, the more senior people said that there would be a massive staff resignation, thus paralyzing the work of the Department of Justice. Faced with this pressure, the Report quotes the President as saying he would not appoint Clark to the position.

Calling Radical Groups to Washington
on January 6, 2021

The linchpin and culmination of the President's plan to overturn the results of the 2020 election was to call disparate groups of radical people, some that used very violent and heated rhetoric, to Washington DC on January 6 and, in an impassioned 70-minute speech on the Ellipse (near the White House) urge them to "fight" for the country. He then instructed them to walk to the Capitol, two miles away, where the Joint Session of Congress had convened about the time the President finished his speech.

This "calling" of groups to the Capitol started with a tweet from the President early on the morning of December 19 and culminated with the Ellipse speech on January 6 from noon – 1:10 p.m. The Committee lists several groups that showed up: Proud Boys, Oath Keepers, Three Percenters, California Patriots—DC Brigade, Florida Guardians of Freedom, QAnon, Groypers and others. In addition, many unaffiliated individual protesters descended on Washington DC for the events.

The language the Committee felt was most inflammatory was the President's mention in his December 19 tweet that things were going to get "wild" in Washington DC, and then his mention in multiple places in his Ellipse speech of the need to "fight for" or "take back" the country. The Committee quotes the President as saying, "Because you'll never take back our country with weakness. You have to show strength and you have to be strong. . .and we fight. We fight like hell. And if you don't fight like hell, you're not going to have a country anymore."

This language stirred up the crowd that eventually made it to the US Capitol. Hard numbers of attendees at the Ellipse speech are hard to come by (the Report on one occasion mentioned about a total of 50,000 people inside and outside the Ellipse), and the numbers actually occupying the Capitol are even more difficult to estimate. But the rest of the Executive Summary relating to this point describes the occupation of the Capitol grounds, beginning just before 1:00 p.m., the illegal entry into the Capitol building about 2:10 p.m. and finally the clearing of the Capitol around 5:00 p.m. after law enforcement got the upper hand. Then the Report describes what it calls President Trump's "187 Minutes of Dereliction of Duty (1:10 p.m. – 4:17 p.m.) where he returned to the White House and did nothing to call off the protesters that were occupying the Capitol.

Questions for Discussion and Further Investigation

1. If you were a Republican in one of the states called for Joe Biden but were told that the election results were likely fraudulent, and that the Republican Party wanted to submit your name as an "alternative" elector because the election results were tainted, what might your reaction have been?

2. If you were in the crowd at the Ellipse on January 6, 2021 and heard the President say what he is quoted as saying in this chapter, would you have marched down to the Capitol when he was finished? What would you have done there had you seen people breaking down the fence around the Capitol? Join them? Leave? Something else?

3. The "fake elector" strategy, as the Committee calls it, was the brainchild of attorney Kenneth Chesebro. Find out what you can about him and his theory.

4. Find a video or several videos online of the occupation of the Capitol. Watch them and describe what you saw. Is this dangerous stuff? Much ado about nothing?

CHAPTER 4

The Big Lie

W ITH THIS ESSAY WE BEGIN OUR treatment of the main body of the Committee's Report. Each essay will now consider one chapter, beginning with page 195, "The Big Lie." The Committee makes a multi-pronged but consistent argument throughout this chapter—that President Trump would do nearly anything, including ignoring the counsel of his closest advisors, to promote a theory that the Presidential election was rife with fraud and that the results of the election unjustly gave the victory to Joe Biden. This "Big Lie" strategy, amply documented in the Report, consisted of several things:

First, the President concluded even before election day that he would refuse to admit possible defeat and that he would contest the results of the election. He also had been told that on Election Day and the days thereafter the nature of Presidential elections could be called a "Red Mirage." This means that, in general, Republicans ("Red") voted in person on election day and their votes were counted immediately. Democrats, generally, used mail-in balloting and their votes were counted afterwards.

Thus, the initial results (counted immediately) would favor the President, but his lead would gradually shrink as (mail-in) ballots were counted into the night and then in the days after election day. The "Red" victory would gradually recede. It was the "Red Mirage." In the middle of the initial surge of "Red" votes, around 2:20 a.m. on the early morning after Election Day, the President declared victory. None of his advisors supported this move. When his lead began to evaporate the next day, as expected, his cries changed from a victory cry to one of election fraud. The report goes into great detail to show that the President's strategy was already decided on well before election day.

Second, when the Networks all called the Presidential election for Joe Biden on Saturday, November 7 (four days after election day), the legal strategy kicked in. Over the next six weeks, Trump supporters filed more than 60 cases in seven battleground states finding fault with various aspects of the elections process. Each suit was designed to cast doubt about the security and accuracy of the voting system in the United States. When the dust had settled, by mid-December, Trump had lost all but one of those cases, many of them presided over by Trump-appointed judges. The Report reviews a case from each of the six most highly contested states to show how judges uniformly condemned the legal filings as more speculative than fact-driven. Contrary to the contentions of many people, factual hearings were granted in more than two dozen of the cases.

These cases were pursued by a legal team headed by former New York City Mayor and Republican Presidential candidate (2008) Rudy Giuliani. His role as a gritty and courageous mayor who inspired New York City back to health after the vicious 9/11 terrorist attacks won him praise at that time from all parties. But taking on this many cases in so short of a period certainly overstretched his resources. Also, as the Report shows, when the rhetoric of a stolen election with no instance of fraud actually demonstrated in a courtroom heated up, many of the main-line law firms across the country which had supported Trump through the election quietly withdrew from representing him. The result was an increasingly narrow field of attorneys who, as judge after judge said, were long on theory but short on facts. Thus, the losses in so many cases become explicable.

Third, after the legal strategy came up empty, by mid-December, the Trump team began to promote the theory of how Dominion voting machines could easily be manipulated to switch votes from Trump to Biden. These machines, they argued, corrupted the election. Every state official who weighed in on the issue testified to the consistency and accuracy of the machines, but that didn't stop the barrage against them. Currently Dominion is pursuing a multi-billion lawsuit against Fox News and others who promoted the theory of faulty voting machines.

Fourth, a series of claims began to surface that many voters voted twice, that more votes than registered voters were cast in some Michigan counties, and that several people who either had moved out of state (Georgia) or who had died were all of a sudden recognized as voters. It was pointed out, somewhat comically, that the lead researcher who presented this Michigan data had misread the prefix of Minnesota (MN) for Michigan (MI) and therefore had Minnesota votes listed as Michigan votes. In addition, what the Committee Report shows is that the first people to investigate these allegations were often the Trump people themselves, who would duly report to the President that the allegations were groundless, a statement that didn't deter the President from continuing to promote his theories of a stolen election, malfunctioning voting machines, and irregular voting patterns. Again, state officials and software experts weighed in and consistently proclaimed the 2020 Presidential election as the "cleanest" on record.

In conclusion, the body of the Committee's report in Chapter One is not only much more extensive than the Executive

Summary, but much more carefully presented and documented. It paints a damning picture of a President who, with the help of Rudy Giuliani and his legal team, consistently tried to erode voter confidence in the fairness of the 2020 Presidential Election. By January 6, 2021, however, when Congress was to meet to certify Joe Biden's victory, the "Big Lie" strategy seemed not to have succeeded. The problem, however, is that a consistent attack on the fairness of a bedrock principle of representative democracy, the ballot box, perhaps injected into the electorate a kind of skepticism of all elections, a feeling that hasn't fully worked its way out of the body politic.

Questions for Discussion and Further Investigation

1. One important point described by the Committee in this section is the "Red Mirage" on Election Day, which has to do with how people vote in America. What is the "Red Mirage" and how does it relate to the "Big Lie?"

2. A strategy of many candidates now who lose close races is to say that "fraud" was involved in "stealing" the election from them. Do you tend to be sympathetic to the claims of those people? Unsympathetic? Should the burden of proof on fairness of elections be placed on those who allege unfairness or on the system that runs the elections?

3. The Trump legal team filed more than 60 cases alleging fraud in various states after the Presidential election. Find out what you can about one or more of those cases.

4. Rudy Giuliani was the President's most vocal lawyer who supported him. Find out what you can about Rudy Giuliani and his role in promoting what the Committee calls the "Big Lie."

CHAPTER 5

I Just Want to Find 11,780 Votes

THE CHAPTER OF THE REPORT ENTITLED "I Just Want to Find 11,780 Votes" tells the story of concerted efforts to pressure state lawmakers between November 7, 2020 and January 6, 2021 to convene special sessions of six legislatures which had been the target of the Trump campaign's efforts (AZ, GA, MI, NM, PA, WI—sometimes NV is also included). These efforts also included attempts to coerce election officials to "find" additional votes for the President.

The thought was that if select legislatures could be re-convened, their task would be fourfold: 1) to declare that fraud in the Presidential election in their state tainted the results; 2) to decertify the tainted results of the election; 3) to exercise their "plenary" power as legislators to name alternate slates of electors; and 4) to make sure that those electors were Trump-supporting electors, inasmuch as the legislatures of these states were controlled by Republicans. Because steps 3 and 4 would likely take some time, the evolving plan of the Trump team also would ask for a delay in ratifying the state vote. This, then, would be presented to Vice-President Mike Pence on January 6 so that, if an outright win would not be proclaimed for President Trump, Pence would have no choice but to grant an extension until the legislatures of these six states could "certify results" that would then lead to new pro-Trump slates of electors.

This strategy, which was greeted by Trump's senior White House legal staff as laughable and crazy, began to gain steam when the engine behind it was Rudy Giuliani and a select core of lawyers, including Jenna Ellis, and very visible and well-connected supporters such as Bernard Kerik, the former NYC Police Commissioner, or Roger Stone. Basic to the effort to get legislatures to be willing to reconvene and pursue this unprecedented strategy, however, was a belief that the election was filled with fraud. As days went on the rhetoric ratcheted up, and on more than one occasion President Trump was quoted saying that this was the most corrupt election in our nation's history.

The major problem faced by this energetic effort to get legislatures in these six states to reconvene, was that none of the legal cases had discovered any 'outcome-determinative' fraud in balloting, and no problems with voting machines had been demonstrated. The case for fraud was often put together out of the flimsiest of narratives and was buttressed with pictures or even a video on one occasion (the so-called "State Farm" video was later shown to have been spliced to make a point that the full video wouldn't support) that supposedly showed ballot drops in the middle of the night or election workers running ballots supporting Biden through the voting machines multiple times.

Yet, the effort to get state legislators to admit that fraud was massive in their state actually won many "converts." The Trump campaign targeted two kinds of legislators: those who had the clout to call special sessions or move the vote along, and those who were characterized as "vulnerable" and perhaps, through some high-level schmoozing or visibility, might become less "vulnerable." During the course of these eight weeks, the President invited hundreds of legislators to the White House so that he could more personally explain why the results of the election had to be reversed and why these legislators were crucial in that effort.

Perhaps the most famous (or infamous) attempt of the President to pressure state officials was his January 2, 2021 phone call to Georgia Secretary of State Brad Raffensperger (a Republican) in which the President went through a litany of election fraud theories which, in turn, were refuted by Raffensperger, and then the President basically said, 'Just find me 11,000 votes' (the margin of his loss in Georgia).

The pressure on several levels of state officials was relentless and verbally abusive. Not only did Trump and his people target those in the executive branches of the states, such as Raffensperger, but legislators in these six states were relentlessly targeted to support efforts to declare their state election results invalid. In addition, the President himself, as well as others, even attacked by name rather low-level elections officials. One particularly egregious case was the attack of Rudy Giuliani, followed up by the President, on two African-American election workers in Georgia, a mother and a daughter. Giuliani made not-so-veiled racist remarks about the two exchanging USB drives as if they were "vials of heroin", when the mother was just passing along a ginger mint to her daughter. The two workers both testified to the Committee that after being so attacked by Rudy Giuliani and the President that they feared for their safety and mental health.

This pressure strategy was developed by former Chapman University law professor John Eastman. It assumed that the state legislatures could simply nullify the results of an election because of suspicion of fraud. But the problem faced by this strategy or theory is that all states have laws that provide for the naming of electors during the state certification of the vote. Once the vote is certified, which it was in almost all cases a few days or weeks after the election, state law doesn't permit the replacement or nullification of the vote. Of course, each state has its own election laws, but no state allows the replacement and naming of new slates of electors simply because the majority of the legislature might believe or assert that the results of the election were fraudulent.

Thus, the Committee argues that the legal theory underlying the vigorous and vicious challenges to the voting in these six states was flawed from the beginning. But, after a failed legal strategy in the courtroom, this was the preferred option: to convince state legislators that they had the power to decertify the results of their state elections.

Ultimately, no state legislature took the Presidential and "Giulianic" bait. In addition to the problem of state laws not permitting the "un-naming" or decertifying of slates of electors, most states had strict rules about the convening of special sessions of their legislatures. It couldn't just happen at the snap of anyone's fingers. Usually the Governor of the state had to call it at the urging of several legislators. Thus, when Republican Governors Ducey of AZ and Kemp of GA refused to do so, they became special enemies of the President.

But this essay has now gone on long enough; it is enough to say that what the Committee describes in great detail in this chapter are the concerted efforts to challenge the integrity of the vote in several states and to develop a (flimsy) theory about challenging the electors.

Questions for Discussion and Further Investigation

1. Should the state legislature be able to nullify the vote of the people of the state for President if they believe there are credible allegations of fraud? What constitutes a "credible allegation of fraud"?

2. The chapter title is taken from a conversation between President Trump and Georgia Secretary of State Brad Raffensperger on January 2, 2021. Find out all you can about that phone conversation and report on it.

3. Take one state (Arizona, Georgia, Michigan, Nevada, New Mexico, Pennsylvania, Wisconsin) and study the strategy used by pro-Trump forces try to find fraud in the 2020 election in that state.

4. Professor Eastman wrote a memo entitled "The Constitutional Authority of State Legislatures to Choose Electors," that was crucial in the effort to try to call special sessions of the legislatures of battleground states in order to reappoint electors. What did this memo say?

CHAPTER 6

The Fake Elector Strategy

S o far, the main body of the report has mentioned three strategies used by the Trump team after the electoral loss on November 3, 2020 to try to overturn the results of that election. The first was a public relations strategy (called by the report "The Big Lie"), in which several people, with the President as chief representative, constantly and insistently claimed that there was massive fraud in several key battleground states (AZ, GA, MI, NV, NM, PA, WI—sometimes six and sometimes seven states are listed). The second strategy was in the legal arena, in which more than 60 challenges to the election were brought in state and federal courts. As mentioned, the Committee doesn't focus on these legal challenges in its Report since another group, coming to similar conclusions, had just released *Lost, Not Stolen* (available on the Internet) in July 2022. The third strategy was a high-pressure campaign, where the President directed efforts against state lawmakers and election officials to find votes or to agree with his claim that the vote was tainted in that state.

The fourth challenge, documented in this brief chapter, was the effort to submit alternative slates of electors (which the report calls "fake electors") to the Vice President so that he might see two potentially conflicting slates of electors from these six or seven states on January 6, 2021, halt the counting of electoral votes, and either remove that state from the electoral count or refer the matter back to state legislatures where questions of fraud had been raised. These legislatures, it was hoped, would eventually return a victory for Trump.

The problematic nature of this effort on its face should be recognized at the outset. I use that word because of the nature of the elections process for President in the United States. In the Presidential election of November 3, 2020, voters cast their votes in the 50 states and the District of Columbia for a President/ Vice-President ticket, but what they really were doing was voting for the electors who would convene six weeks later (December 14, 2020) to cast their electoral votes in their state Capitols for the winning ticket in the state.

Slates of electors had been drawn up by the respective political parties in anticipation of victory, but when a candidate won at the polls, only his electors were certified by the state elections officials. The date for certification of victory differed in every state, but December 14 was the date set by law for official casting of electoral votes. Once this was done, a "Certificate of Ascertainment" was issued and signed by the Secretary of State and Governor, combined with a "Certificate of Vote" which listed the votes for each Presidential candidate for that state. These, stamped with the state seal, would then be forwarded to many places, among them the National Archives and the US Senate and House.

Thus, by December 14, 2020, well after each state had called its winner, the electoral votes in all jurisdictions were duly cast and certified, and Certificates of Ascertainment were sent to Congress and the National Archives. These gave the names of the valid electors of the state.

The strategy developed by the Trump team would not say that these slates of obviously valid electoral votes were per se invalid, but they would claim that challenges to the validity of election results meant that standby or alternative slates of electors of the Republican party (the Republican candidate—Trump—lost in each one of these seven states) would be held contingently just in case a court decided to support a legal challenge or sent the issue to the state legislatures for their determination. This theory rested on the idea that the state legislature, rather than the people of the state, had the ultimate authority to choose electors.

This theory, as the Committee details, was developed by attorney Kenneth Chesebro [the report doesn't indicate clearly there relationship between Chesebro and Eastman]. Its first iteration, articulated in mid-November 2020, only stated that these alternative slates were contingent, that is, only should be available if a court decision made it necessary to have an alternative slate at the ready. But Chesebro wrote two more memos in December that gradually abandoned that theory and just argued for the legitimacy of alternative electors so that it would potentially cause confusion to the Vice-President on January 6, when the electoral certificates were opened and counted, and that this confusion would buy an additional two weeks to convince state legislatures that they indeed had the power to declare who won the Presidential election in their states. Since the legislatures in the contested states were controlled by Republicans, it was easy to surmise that a confused Vice-President on January 6 would refer the matter back to the States, that Republican State Legislatures would intervene and then declare the results for Trump.

The major problem with this theory was that the alternative electors never had official "Certificates of Ascertainment" issued for them—that is, there was no legal way for them to be recognized as legitimate electors, and that the allegations of fraud in the election were merely allegations—and had been demonstrated in no court of law.

The problematic nature (a term I used earlier) of the alternative elector scenario, and the pro-Trump effort to name alternative electors and have them considered legitimate, even without a Certificate of Ascertainment, might be best understood by a hypothetical. Say that the local Odd Fellows or Kiwanis Chapter decided, to liven up one of their monthly socials, to name a slate of electors, all of the same party, declare themselves a surrogate for the state Republican party, copy the way that official notices were sent to the Congress and National Archives, and then forward the "Kiwanis" or "Odd Fellows Republican Slate" as the "duly chosen" electors of the state. Would anyone believe you had a legitimate second slate of electors?

In addition, on December 11, 2020 the US Supreme Court dealt a blow to those supporting the false elector theory when it dismissed a legal challenge from Texas which claimed that the voting practices in several other states were not legal. The Supreme Court quickly saw that wading into this morass of States questioning the validity of other States' voting practices would be a recipe for quick dissolution of the Republic, and they dismissed the case with a 9-0 vote.

As mentioned, these "fake electors" slates were duly forwarded to the Congress and the National Archives. As expected, these submissions of alternative slates of electors were rejected by the US Senate Parliamentarian because they were not submitted in accordance with law. An unsolved legal question at this time is whether those people who signed their names on the alternative electoral certificates, in which they claimed to be the true electors, might face any legal consequences.

Questions for Discussion and Further Investigation

1. What is the Electoral College and how does it work?
2. One can win the Presidential election in the United States and lose the popular vote. How could this happen? Should the Presidential election be based on the Electoral College system or direct popular vote?
3. What is a "Certificate of Ascertainment" and what is its role in the establishing the electors from a state?
4. If you were the US Senate Parliamentarian, and you received a supposed slate of electors from a slate but it didn't have the "official" markings, such as the Governor's signature or the state seal, what might you do?

CHAPTER 7

"Just Call it Corrupt"—President Trump's Effort to Co-opt the Federal Department of Justice

THIS CHAPTER DISCUSSES A FIFTH STRATEGY, beginning a few weeks after the election, to try to bring the US Department of Justice into the picture. The eventual goal was to pressure the Department to draft a letter to the state legislatures in battleground states indicating that the Department had evidence of voter fraud and that the Department strongly recommended calling of Special Sessions that might lead to overriding the Election Day vote of the people of those states. By the time we get to this part of the strategy we can see patterns that have developed. First, have a basic theory that guides all your action (massive vote fraud); second, call for an "undoing" of the vote in those states where massive fraud was alleged; third, submit either an alternative slate of electors or, preferably, authorize a decision by the state legislature (controlled by Republicans in each of these states) to vote on a new slate of electors (certainly

Republican) and, finally, submit either conflicting slates or just the new Republican slate to Congress for approval on January 6.

As should be evident, however, the major hurdles that this general theory and its implementation needed to overcome were twofold: a) That the states had certified their votes, and that the electoral college had cast its vote on December 14 for Joe Biden for President. On December 14, he received 306 electoral votes to Donald Trump's 232. Thus, Biden received many more than the 270 needed to clinch the election; and b) That no instance of outcome-determinative fraud had been demonstrated. If there were irregularities in voting, meaning that a hand recount didn't tally perfectly with the voting machine totals, it was usually in the handful of votes (rather than thousands) and could most likely be attributed to human error. That is, there was no evidence of outcome-determinative fraud, or defective voting machines, despite example after example of supposed fraud endlessly coming from the mouths of President Trump and his most trusted lieutenants.

Before discussing briefly the effort to pressure and co-opt the Department of Justice into declaring massive election problems, a word should be said about conspiratorial thinking (this is my editorializing, and isn't in the report). In my experience it is quite easy to assert that any human system, governmental or otherwise, is "corrupt." It is also very easy to bring supposed evidence of corruption, based on information that cannot easily be verified by the hearers. "I know they are all on the take!" a person screamed to me, while arguing that the entire American system is "corrupt" and has to come down. Other than patiently trying to answer allegations, which sometimes multiply like rabbits in the springtime, those on the receiving end of conspiratorial thinkers are at a loss. Often the only hope is that there are places where evidence needs to be brought forward and judged, but usually the conspiratorial thinkers are loath to show up in those forums.

But conspiratorial thinking definitely infected the Trump Administration in the days following the November 3, 2020 Presidential election. Votes had been stolen from one state and given to another; elections division workers double-counted Democratic votes; ballot "dumps" in the middle of the night gave an unfair advantage to Biden; the voting machines were controlled by foreign entities that easily could switch a Trump vote to a Biden vote. All of these allegations were presented with the aim of eroding trust in the American electoral system.

This chapter describes the effort to get the US Department of Justice to declare that massive fraud corrupted the 2020 Presidential Election. President Trump was not pleased with the Department ever since his hand-picked Attorney General, William Barr, said to an Associated Press reporter on December 1, 2020 that there was no evidence of massive election fraud. This interview with the reporter, which countered the narrative Trump was giving, eventually led to Barr's resignation from the Department the week before Christmas 2020. This decision to resign (he wasn't fired) has made me wonder. . .Why didn't Barr stick it out for three more weeks, when sticking it out would have been a powerful counterweight to Trump's efforts to co-opt the Department?

In any case, President Trump was relentless in trying to get the Department to declare fraud in the elections. The Department had two problems with this. First, they had examined, along with the FBI, numerous allegations of voter fraud and also had concluded that there was nothing to the allegations and, second, they had very limited jurisdiction in federal elections—elections were largely the province of the states. The biggest threat to the independence of the Department of Justice came early in 2021 (Jan 2-4) when Trump planned to appoint a low-level employee of the Department, who believed in and supported his conspiracy theories, to be the Acting Attorney General. Once in this position, this person (Jeffrey

Clark) would have sent out a letter to several states urging them to "Hold everything!" because the Department had uncovered patterns of electoral fraud. The senior Department officials told the President that he could, of course, fire them, and appoint Clark as Acting Attorney General but that all of the Associate and Assistant Attorneys General would resign *en masse*, because it would be obvious that the President was trying to politicize the Department. Only this threat made the President back off.

So, President Trump's strategy of trying to corrupt the Department of Justice by having them be an arm of his conspiratorial thinking failed. But, as this chapter demonstrates, it didn't fail by much. So determined, and so forthright, was President Trump that nothing else than getting a reversal of the 2020 Presidential election results mattered.

Questions for Discussion and Further Investigation

1. You are Attorney General William Barr and have been fully loyal to the President since you were appointed in February 2019. You looked into allegations of fraud in the Presidential election of 2020 and came up with nothing significant. The President wants you to get on board with him. What do you do?

2. Define and describe the nature of conspiracy thinking or conspiratorial thinking. What makes a person a "conspiracy theorist?"

3. Research and report on the tense discussions between the President and his Acting Attorney General Jeffrey Rosen in the early days of January 2021 on the subject of voter fraud.

4. What might have been the result if President Trump had appointed Jeffrey Clark as Acting Attorney General early in 2021 and he had sent out letters to the states saying that the Federal Department of Justice had evidence of voter fraud in the Presidential election?

Chapter 8

Pressuring Vice-President Mike Pence

THE FIVE-FOLD STRATEGY TO OVERTURN THE results of the 2020 Presidential Election, described in previous essays, was not working. With each passing week, and with each new affirmation of the finality of the election results, President Trump's options were fewer. The calendar was rushing towards January 6, the day when Congress would certify or officially count the electoral votes. Finality in the election, it seemed, was soon going to happen.

Contributing to that growing sense of finality were several things. First, there was the unanimous call of the election for Joe Biden by the all major networks on November 7, 2020; second was the certification of the election in each state on different dates according to its own laws; third was the casting of electoral ballots on December 14, 2020 in each state Capitol. The Governors of each state then sent certificates, called Certificates of Ascertainment, to the President of the Senate (i.e., the Vice-President in his Congressional role) and the National Archives, among others. These were the verified or valid electors from each state.

That date, December 14, 2020, should then have sealed or finalized the Presidential vote. The final electoral tally was 306 for Biden and 232 for Trump. It was a respectable, but not overwhelming, victory for Biden. It was somewhat stunning for Trump because, after all, he was the incumbent and fully expected on January 1, 2020 to be re-elected, perhaps by a wide margin. But by the end of 2020 Trump and his team refused not only to concede the election but continued to argue that the election was "stolen," that voting machines were defective, and that the most massive fraud in the history of Presidential elections was perpetrated leading up to, on, and following November 3, 2020. Because Trump decided to continue to fight, he had to decide on another theory and course of action to try to overturn the results. The theory was supplied by law professor John Eastman, and it related to the powers of the Vice-President in the counting of the electoral votes in the Joint Session of Congress on January 6, 2021.

Ever since the 12th Amendment to the US Constitution (early 19th century) and the Electoral Count Act of 1887 were passed, there was a shared understanding of the Vice-President's role in counting the votes on January 6. Though the language of the Amendment is very brief, and that of Section 15 of the Electoral Count Act (codified at 3 USC 15) is ambiguous at certain important points, it had unanimously been understood that the Vice-President's role in counting the votes was merely ministerial. That is, he was to open the envelopes from each of the states, give the envelopes to clerks who were appointed by the two chambers of Congress, receive the tally of the electoral votes from the clerks and announce that count to the Congress. Whoever of the candidates for President got 270 or more electoral votes would be the next President. That was the Vice-President's role. To accept and announce the count of electoral votes. This ministerial function of the Vice-President (acting as President of the Senate) was also accepted universally because imagining a substantive power of the Vice-President at this point would be like giving to one man a role very much like a "king-maker." To a new country in 1776 or 1787 bristling at the idea of royal leadership under George III, this thought would not only be counterintuitive but ridiculous.

Yet, over the course of about six weeks, from late November 2020 to early January 2021, Professor Eastman devised a two-fold strategy (sometimes it looked like a three-fold strategy) that would enable the Vice-President to be the one to determine the next President of the United States. Here is how it worked: Eastman told the President, in two memos, that the Vice-President had substantive power to do two things on January 6. He could (1) refuse to accept the electoral votes of states where there was more than one slate of electors presented to him (recall a previous essay on the strategy of the Republicans to create alternative slates of electors, which the report consistently calls "fake electors"); or (2) he could say that there were reports of widespread fraud and that therefore the electoral tallies needed to be returned to the state legislatures so that they could "investigate" the reports of fraud and come back with fresh slates of electors within ten days. Since the state legislatures were controlled 27-22 by Republicans (with one tie), the assumption was that a majority of Republican slates of electors would be returned. Under either scenario, Pence would eventually name Trump as President for a second term.

Even the mere mention of both of these theories made the President's senior lawyers, Cipillone and Herschmann, cringe. They knew that such theories were not only pulled out of thin air, but had no historical precedent and would open the door for massive electoral chaos. They also knew that to disallow a vote in various states, like Arizona, because there were supposedly competing slates of electors, ignored the fact that the Republican-submitted slate was really a "shadow" slate—not done with the

Seal of the State, the approval of the Governor or the following of state processes. In a word, they were sham slates. To expect the Vice-President now to assume powers that a Vice-President never had assumed, and then to put into effect a legal theory that assumed that fake slates were just as legitimate as certified slates, would have been mind-boggling. Not one Republican would agree to give Kamala Harris those powers in 2025.

Pause for a minute and imagine a scenario on January 6, 2025 if a Republican seemingly won the Presidential Election in 2024. President of the Senate Kamala Harris could look at the state electoral tallies and say on January 6, 2025, "Hm...I smell a rat. I think I want to disallow Wyoming, Kansas, Florida, Nebraska and any other state the Republicans won. Oh. . .second term for Biden." No one in their right mind could assume the legitimacy such a scenario. Yet, that, according to the Report, was precisely what Mike Pence was being pressured to do.

The chapter ends on a sad and even scary note. Not only did President Trump daily ratchet up the pressure on Pence to act in this illegal way but he even, as it were, released his followers against him, especially with his 2:24 p.m. tweet on January 6 saying to his followers that "Mike Pence has let us down." The Capitol was breached in the moments immediately before and after that text.

The sobering results of this chapter are that the President put the lives of many, including his own Vice-President, at risk because of his unremitting effort to overturn the election. The one point that should be mentioned, however, is that late in 2022 the Congress "updated" the Electoral Count Act of 1887. Though even in its original form it gave no substantive powers to the Vice-President in counting the electoral votes, there really are enough ambiguities and dated language in the text to allow for different interpretations of what an "objection" is to the vote count. There doesn't seem to be much question, however, that what the

President was asking, really demanding that Vice-President Pence do was illegal, unconstitutional and unprecedented.

Questions for Discussion and Further Investigation

1. As mentioned, the electoral tally on January 6 was 306-232, with Biden winning. If the electoral votes from the seven contested states (AZ, GA, MI, NM, NV, PA, WI) were disallowed, how would that have affected the electoral college results?
2. The chapter cites President Trump repeatedly claiming that Vice-President Pence had the power to deliver another four years in the White House to him. What does that assume about the Vice-President's role on January 6?
3. Look up, read about, and describe Professor Eastman's theory about why the Vice-President had power on January 6 to disallow the electoral votes of certain states or remand the whole issue of electoral voting back to the state legislatures.
4. Read section 15 of the Electoral Count Act of 1887, cited above, and then study how Congress "updated" the Act in 2022. What did you find?

CHAPTER 9

Calling People to Washington DC on January 6, 2021

CHAPTER SIX OF THE MAIN REPORT, the subject of this chapter, is hard to read for two reasons. First, it is so filled with quotations and footnotes, discussing how leaders of various movements who were present at the occupation of the US Capitol were communicating with each other between December 19, 2020 and January 6, 2021 that a continuous narrative is hard to present. Second, it is hard to read because it consists of such inflammatory and insurrectionary rhetoric against the legitimate winner of the Presidential election and the Congress that would certify that result. Language of death and killing, of building gallows, of obliteration of opponents, of storming the Capitol, of leading another revolution is dripping from text after text of those who came to the Capitol during the January 6, 2021 certification.

What is particularly poignant and powerful for the Committee, however, is that this violent and revolutionary language arises from a disparate group of Americans who were without question called to Washington DC by President Trump.

The "offending tweet" that got everything started came from the President a little after 1:30 a.m. on Saturday December 19, 2020. He had just finished a meeting in which, as his lawyers would later describe, the "clown car" or the proponents of conspiracy theories got the upper hand with the President in supporting a movement to do something "wild" on January 6. And so, in the dim hours of that Saturday morning, the President urged his followers by Twitter that there would a "Big protest in D.C. on January 6. Be there, will be wild!"

And so it was. This chapter lays out the "wildness" that followed the call of the President to Washington DC. Obviously, as the various texts and postings of members of the radical groups that responded to his text show, this "wild" reference had to do with people doing all in their power to "stop the steal" and prevent the Congress from certifying the victory of Joe Biden.

Most of the chapter is concerned with describing the various radical groups that responded to the President's call—giving a brief history of the group; introducing its leading characters; showing what role they played in the lead-up to January 6. This call to the various groups, and their frantic and frenetic efforts to comply with the call with but 2 1/2 weeks of notice culminated in the hour before the actual occupation of the Capitol building with President Trump's address to the assembled crowds at the Ellipse on January 6 at noon. In his 70-minute address he urged his followers, many of whom stayed outside the Ellipse because they didn't want to pass through the metal detectors, which would have exposed weapons, to "fight like hell" for the future of the country. People who have examined his actual speech report that he used the verb "fight" at least twenty times, though the prepared text of his remark used it fewer than five times. If his followers didn't "fight like hell," they would no longer have a country. That was the substance of his message.

It might be useful to list some of the groups and personalities whom the President inspired to "be wild." There was the "Stop the Steal" coalition, a group that long-standing Trump ally Roger Stone (who had just been pardoned by the President in December 2020 for crimes related to the 2016 Presidential election) said should be building an army of lawyers and suing "like there's no tomorrow." One of the key allies of the "Stop the Steal" movement was conspiracy theorist Alex Jones. Jones, famous for his rhetoric insulting and assaulting the families of children mowed down in the Sandy Hook killings in December 2012, mixed a potent cocktail of allegations of election fraud and imminent demise of America if the election went to Joe Biden.

But with the President tweeting the need for his radical followers to come to DC on January 6 to "be wild," he was able for one brief moment to unite many disparate groups with the goal of not allowing Congress to certify the results of the election. These groups included the more decentralized Proud Boys; the "top-down" Oath Keepers, the white nationalist Groypers led by Nick Fuentes, the QAnon conspiracists, and the Three Percenters, so named because of the now generally debunked notion that it only took three percent of colonists in 1776 to overthrow the British rule. Each of them was quite different from each other; indeed Stewart Rhodes, the leader of the Oath Keepers couldn't stand QAnon but, since the Commander-in-Chief had called them together in this moment of dire national emergency, as they saw it, they would unite forces.

The common theme of these groups, to repeat, is that the election was stolen, and that the country had to be taken back from those who had stolen the election. The groups coming to Washington DC were coming to make sure, to the best of their ability, that the electoral votes weren't ratified by Congress. There was some talk about having the vote return to the state legislatures, but all those niceties were lost in the searing heat of protest. This was 1776 again! This was the storming of the Bastille in the 21st century! This was the invasion of the Winter Palace in 1917 by the Bolsheviks! This would finally be the time when the PEOPLE will speak!

That, or something very like that, was the rhetoric that fueled the disparate group of protesters who descended on the Capitol on January 6. And, the composer and conductor of the great symphony of action was President Donald Trump. That is the burden of this chapter of the Committee Report.

Questions for Discussion and Further Investigation

1. If you believed the President that the election had been "stolen" from him, and then he tweeted you to come to Washington on January 6 because it would be "wild," would you be inclined to come? What would you be ready to do?
2. Imagine yourself coming to the Capitol to protest the election on January 6, but you are a peaceful person and just want to make your voice "heard." How would you respond if you heard some of your fellow protesters uttering the more violent rhetoric described above?
3. Choose one of the groups whom President Trump called to the Capitol on January 6, research its beliefs and history, and report back. If you already chose one on an earlier question, select another.
4. Find and read a copy of President Trump's Ellipse speech at noon on January 6. How would you characterize the speech?

Chapter 10

187 Minutes of Dereliction of Duty

T HE "187 Minutes" in the title of Chapter Seven of the Committee Report points to the three hours and seven minutes from the time that President Trump finished his Ellipse speech (1:10 p.m.) until he finally called off his supporters from occupying the Capitol and trying to prevent the Congress from doing its job of certifying the Presidential election results (4:17 p.m.). The Committee calls it a "dereliction of duty" because it is drawing on US military terminology where dereliction of duty is defined as when a "person willfully or negligently fails to perform that person's duties or when that person performs them in a culpably inefficient manner."

The point of the Committee in this chapter is that this definition of "dereliction of duty" accurately characterizes the cavalier and indifferent attitude of the President in the hours when the attack on and occupation of the Capitol was taking place. The President, at any time after being informed that there was an occupation of the Capitol (about 1:20 p.m.), could have told the protesters to stop what they were doing and go home. They would have obeyed him. As was evident when he ultimately did this, at 4:17 p.m., they (the occupiers) complied and dispersed within the hour. They said, in tweets later discovered by the Committee, that they were simply following orders of their Commander-in-Chief.

The crowd that entered the Capitol, caused considerable damage, and temporarily prevented Congress from doing its job had been:

- called there by President Trump, beginning with a December 19 early morning tweet;
- egged on by President Trump in a 70- minute speech at the Ellipse just before and after the Capitol grounds were breached by the protesters on January 6; and
- inflamed by the President in a 2:24 p.m. tweet that condemned Vice-President Pence for not acting on the discredited legal theory of John Eastman to stop the vote count and refer the re-selection of electors back to the state legislatures.

Three additional points of special importance in order to understand the flow of this chapter and the 187 minutes are: first, the refusal of the Secret Service to allow President Trump to go to the Capitol personally after his Ellipse speech ended at 1:10 p.m.; second, the escalation of violence in the Capitol after the President tweeted his disapproval of Vice-President Pence's ignoring his words to nullify the election at 2:24 p.m.; and, third, the persistent and consistent refusal of the President to acknowledge tweets even by his greatest supporters, to call for an end to the occupation until it became clear that enough police had arrived on the scene to outnumber the protesters. A word about each will focus the discussion.

First. On more than one occasion during his Ellipse speech, where the President also urged the crowd to "fight" more than twenty times, he mentioned to the assembled crowd that he would be joining them at the Capitol at the conclusion of his speech. It should be noted that the crowd inside the Ellipse was estimated at about 27,000, with another 25,000 standing nearby because they refused to pass through the metal detectors, most likely because they didn't want weapons confiscated. Many who heard him say he would join the protesters knew that these words presaged immense trouble, because what would most likely have happened next is to set up some kind of makeshift stage at the Capitol to "direct" the protesters in their actions—thus inflaming tensions even more. But the Secret Service refused to take him to the Capitol, citing concerns with providing security, even though the President argued that they were *his* people and were not out to hurt *him*. Many pages of the report deal with silence or some conflicting statements of witnesses about how hot the discussion became between the President and the Secret Service when they refused to take him to the Capitol building. In retrospect, that decision probably saved the Republic from an even greater toll of damage that day.

Second. The protesters breached security lines surrounding the Capitol for the first time just before 1:00 p.m. and entered the Capitol at about 2:15 p.m. on Wednesday, January 6. Congress had convened at 1:00 p.m. to certify the election results. From about 2:15-3:15 p.m. there was chaos as Congress gradually became aware of the growing din outside their walls, adjourned their meeting, sought cover in the growing smoke and gloom (they were issued gas masks) and escaped to secure locations. But then, at 2:24 p.m., the President sent the following tweet, "Mike Pence didn't have the courage to do what should have been done to protect our Country and our Constitution, giving States a chance to certify a corrected set of facts, not the fraudulent or inaccurate ones. . . " This tweet added fuel to the fire of the crowd's already threatening actions. They overran the police lines, swarmed the Capitol, came within 40' of encountering the fleeing party of

Vice-President Mike Pence, and generally had a field day that was captured and circulated on countless videos. As one protester later said, "It was awesome!"

Third. With the increased violence being broadcast live, a great number of people, including Trump's biggest supporters in his family and on Fox News, all sent him texts urging, even begging him to call off the protesters. Many stated their advice in crassly political terms, that the continuation of the protest would damage his legacy. Though there may have been some in the White House who were urging the opposite, the Committee gives no texts of supporters who thought that the occupation of the Capitol was a good thing. Only the President seemed to be unconcerned, letting matters continue to unravel until slightly after 4:00 p.m. Then he arose from watching Fox News to film a four-minute video urging his supporters to withdraw and go home. His words to them were not ones of disapproval or anger, but rather of disappointment. He said, among other things: "Go home. We love you. You are special." As the committee points out, never once in that day did the President inquire after the well-being of his Vice-President or consult with military or other officials who would have quickly restored order. This is why the Select Committee calls this chapter a "dereliction of duty."

As President Trump's daughter Ivanka said in testimony to the Select Committee, her father didn't want to talk about the event after it was over. He didn't seem to express any remorse for it. Within two days it was "over" for him. . .Until the work of the Select Committee.

Questions for Discussion and Further Investigation

1. If in fact the Secret Service refused to drive President Trump to the Capitol upon his orders after his Ellipse speech, do you think their refusal was justified? Or, should they have obeyed

the orders of the Commander-in-Chief if he wanted to go to the Capitol?

2. The Committee's major point is that the President *could* have done a lot in those 187 minutes to dispel the crowd but he didn't, and that this is a dereliction of duty because it violated his oath he took to defend the Constitution and Laws of the United States. Do you think that the Committee is just over-reacting and that the President, by calling off his supporters at 4:17 p.m. really was acting responsibly in these three hours and was *not* derelict in his duty?

3. Build a detailed timeline or chronology of the events near the Capitol during the afternoon of January 6, 2021. What in your judgment are the five or six most important events to understand that afternoon?

4. The President's tweet at 2:24 saying that Mike Pence had let them down seemed to add fuel to the protesters' fire. Find that tweet and discuss whether it was inflammatory and irresponsible or in some way was justifiable.

Chapter 11

An Analysis of the Occupation of the Capitol

IN THE PREVIOUS CHAPTER I USED the Committee's description of the period of 1:10-4:17 p.m. on the afternoon of January 6, 2021 as President Trump's "dereliction of duty," because the Committee argues he abandoned his duty to defend the Constitution and Laws of the United States while the US Capitol was being breached. When I summarized those 187 minutes, I focused on President Trump's activity (or, more accurately, inactivity) as he completed his Ellipse speech, dismissed the crowd, urged them to "fight like hell," and then went back to the White House to follow the events on television.

The justification for President Trump's conduct, as has been previously mentioned, was that he claimed the election was "stolen" and that massive "fraud" had been perpetrated on the American people in multiple states. It was, in his words, the most corrupt election in the history of the United States. But by the time January 6, 2021 had rolled around, no convincing proof of this fraud had been forthcoming. He was down to very few options. His multi-pronged strategy to have the election results thrown out had foundered at every turn, even though he exerted considerable effort to get the results thrown out.

The only avenue left to reverse this most horrendous miscarriage of justice, in the minds of President Trump and his most fervent followers, was to call his "troops" to the Capitol on January 6. These people consisted of a motley collection of half-a-dozen or more radical groups detailed elsewhere in these chapters, as well as many "independent" protesters. Though numbers are difficult precisely to ascertain, it appeared that a little over 50,000 supporters either attended or were just outside the grounds of the Ellipse during his speech. Hundreds, and perhaps even thousands more, from the Proud Boys and others, staked out a different route that day, beginning at the Washington Monument, and walking to the Capitol during and before Trump's speech on the Ellipse. Many of the 50,000 listeners didn't actually head down to the Capitol. The only number the Select Committee came up with of those actually breaching the Capitol grounds was 20,000 (with far fewer actually in the Capitol building)—still a very large and scary number.

The burden of this chapter of the Report is to detail the process by which the outer barriers of the Capitol grounds were breached (just before 1:00 p.m.) and then trace the way that three breaches to the actual building, on the East, West and North sides happened, beginning at 2:13 p.m. Ironically, the launching point for the breach from the West side of the Capitol was from a place called "Peace Circle." A second irony is that the breaking into the Capitol building itself happened by those who had climbed up the massive scaffolding that was built on the Northwest side of the Capitol to accommodate the platform for the Presidential inauguration to be held on January 20. That is, the structure that was supposed to witness to the *continuity* of this great experiment in Democracy became the instrument through which the greatest potential *threat* to the Democracy was launched.

But the occupation or "attack" on the Capitol, as the Committee calls it, really began long before the outer barrier surrounding the Capitol was breached just before 1:00 p.m. on January 6. The Committee lays out in detail the instructions given by leaders of radical groups to their members beginning on January 5 and the morning hours of January 6. One of the issues discussed was the nature of weapons that many either were carrying or had brought with them to Washington DC. Because Washington DC had a ban on handgun carry within its borders, there was considerable discussion of alternative weapons to bring (e.g., axes, hockey sticks, flags with pointed tips). In short, many of those inspired by President Trump's rhetoric were looking at the events of January 6 as a way violently to "take back" the country.

The Report then goes on to detail an almost moment-by-moment account of the protesters' taking over the Capitol. First the fence on the West side was trampled. Then, the surging of protesters. Then, the overrunning of police officers. What soon happened was the Capitol Police and Metropolitan Washington DC Police were so vastly outnumbered that they were unable to hold the line. By then President Trump's Ellipse speech had concluded, and a pumped-up band of his supporters added numbers and energy to the Capitol occupation. Some visible personalities, like Alex Jones, egged on the crowd, according to the Report. Then, at about 2:00 p.m. people were climbing on the scaffolding. Then, at 2:13 the breach of the Capitol building itself took place. Crowds of protesters surged inside the Capitol, some taking selfies and posting them on social media (which would later, ironically, be used to arrest them), some occupying the House and Senate chambers, some seemingly aimlessly wandering the spacious halls. The ebb and flow of protesters getting the upper hand and security forces retaking spaces is detailed in the Report. The Report also mentions that the President's tweet at 2:24 p.m. seemed to have given the protesters an additional jolt of energy.

Thus, the Capitol building itself was breached at 2:13 p.m. Both Chambers of Congress were immediately evacuated. Gas masks were given to Members of Congress because tear gas had been fired at protesters and was starting to fog up the halls. The Chambers were then overrun by the protesters by 2:45 p.m. Chaos ensued for about 2 to 2 1/2 hours. In those hours, more than 130 police officers, charged with defending the Capitol, were injured, some seriously. Then, around 5 or 5:15 p.m., the police were able to get the situation back under control and force the protesters out of the Capitol building. The National Guard troops arrived shortly thereafter to secure the Capitol. President Trump sent his video message at 4:17 p.m. telling the protesters that he loved them but it was time for them to go home, and this also contributed to the change in mood. By 5:30 p.m. the protesters had been moved out of the Capitol building and were gradually being expelled from the Capitol grounds.

Questions for Discussion and Further Investigation

1. What would you say to a protester who was not bent on violence that day but simply wanted to enter the Capitol to register his/her disagreement with the certification of the election of Joe Biden, but was subsequently arrested, charged, convicted and sent to prison? Would you sympathize with them if they felt their penalty was unjust?

2. If you were a Congressional staffer or Congress person on duty in the Capitol that day and heard that the grounds of the Capitol and then the building itself were breached, what would have been your reaction?

3. Watch an easily-available online video of the breach of the Capitol grounds or the Capitol building itself. How would you describe what you see?
4. More than 130 Capitol and DC police officers were injured that day in the line of duty. Try to find out the names of some of the injured officers and how they were hurt.

CHAPTER 12

Recommendations and Appendices

IN THIS CHAPTER WE REACH THE end of the Report proper and focus on two of the four Appendices to the Report. The last small section of the Report contains a list of eleven Recommendations, on pp. 689-692. These Recommendations differ from the criminal charges referred to the Special Prosecutor on pp. 103-113 of the Report because the charges are directed to an official overseeing a series of potential criminal charges against former President Trump while the recommendations relate to general ways that the Committee believes that law, training, and accountability of public officials could be improved as a result of the Committee's work.

For example, of the eleven Recommendations made by the Select Committee, three relate to the amendment or interpretation of federal statutes. One is a recommendation to beef up the Electoral Count Act of 1887 to make it more clear that the Vice-President only has ministerial duties to perform on January 6. A law to this effect was enacted by Congress in December

2022. One is an interpretation of the Fourteenth Amendment which would lead to President Trump's inability to stand for election to a federal office again. One raises the issue of whether the Insurrection Act (of 1792), which the Oath Keepers urged the President to use to declare martial law, ought to be modernized. A few of the Recommendations relate to the importance not just of holding the Capitol occupiers legally liable for their action, but also the officials who supported them. Strongly encouraged are actions of state bar committees to disbar or discipline attorneys who fostered illegal schemes which led to the breaching and occupation of the Capitol. Finally, a few of the Recommendations simply seem to bemoan the increase in fringe conspiracy theorist groups and the role of the media in publicizing misleading information that may have stoked fears and illegal activity. These Recommendations would make useful discussion points for group consideration.

The first two Appendices consider the role and preparation of various police or military organizations for the events of January 6. I will spend the rest of this chapter on those Appendices. The final two Appendices are shorter and don't relate to the events of January 6.

Since the Capitol building was breached and overrun for almost three hours on January 6, there needs to be considerable attention to the reasons why law enforcement could not contain the protesters and fully protect Congress in these three hours. One point made in passing in the Report, but not further discussed in the Appendices about law enforcement (Appendices 1-2), was that January 6 was not historically a significant security day on the Hill, which led to less than adequate preparation. Yet, the Committee didn't focus on this issue in its Appendices 1-2. Rather, their focus there was on the nuts and bolts of decisions made (or not made) by the chains of command and the relationship of various police and military units on that day.

Two significant points emerge for me from these 80 pages of discussion and footnotes. The first is that the DC National Guard, which was delayed for more than three hours in arriving on the scene (from about 1:45-5:00 p.m.), and which was eventually crucial in tamping down the final stages of the occupation, was delayed in action not because of willful efforts of anyone to further anyone's political agenda but because of fear. The nature of the fear had nothing to do with the events of January 6, 2021. Rather, it related to events of the previous summer—2020.

To put the issue briefly in perspective: the summer of 2020 was one of the most difficult summers in recent American history. Not only was the country under lockdown because of the Covid-19 Pandemic in most large cities, but protests in the wake of George Floyd's death, which had just happened on May 25, 2020, led to chaos and riots in many American cities. In response to this chaos President Trump was desirous of, and did, send in the National Guard (his advisors dissuaded him from sending in the US Army) to quell the disputes. But this action created enormous divisions not only in the affected cities but in the highest levels of the military establishment overseeing the National Guard. That is, the fear that was generated in the Summer of 2020 was that the US military or a branch of it (the National Guard) might violently turn against (largely unarmed) American citizens. That is NOT what happens in the US. It may happen under other regimes, but not here. That was the fear that gripped the military establishment on January 6, 2021.

So, very deep fear was generated in all levels of the military establishment that when another crucial day would come where the possibility of military deployment *within the borders* of the US might happen, they simply would refuse to or be very reluctant to deploy. And, especially if it had to do with military troops on Capitol Hill—that is a NO! NO! That is what military regimes do. We are a country that believes in the peaceful transition of power.

Now we can see why the DC National Guard, which was the arm of the military that would serve as "backup" if local police forces were strained beyond their limits, would not be called up or would only reluctantly be called up. For just over three crucial hours (from about 1:45 p.m. -5:00 p.m.) on the afternoon of January 6, people within the Capitol building, outside the building, all over called for HELP from the National Guard, but the Guard was "delayed." It was delayed because of fear—fear of repeating the ugly scenes of the summer of 2020 and fear of making America look like it was a state that really was held together by the military.

If that was the principal problem that allowed the occupation of the Capitol to go on for more than three hours, the secondary problem was that the police forces charged with protecting the Capitol were so diverse and under different command that no unified communication and approach to intervening could be decided upon. That is, there was the United States Capitol police, whose job it was to protect the Capitol, joining with the Metropolitan DC police, whose job it was to clean up things outside of the Capitol building, and the United States Park Service Police, whose job it was to police and protect the Mall and other federal park spaces, abundant as they are, in Washington DC. Each one had its chain of command, its modes of communication, its staffing issues, its different training, even its different approach to arming troops.

Let it be said here that from all I have read the line officers performed with utmost professionalism and skill, but they were hampered by conflicting reports coming from their higher-ups. That is, some high in the chain of command felt that the "vibe" picked up from social media and other sources said that January 6 was going to be a violent day. Others thought it was going to be 'sorta bad' but 'our boys' were really good at handling problems. So, there were different assessments of how dangerous the situation was going to be.

Coupled with this problem was a lack of real-time coordination, so that when breaches actually happened at the North side of the Capitol building at 2:13 p.m. and thereafter, there were not many officers to fight off the surging crowds. The police were outnumbered, and they weren't properly deployed. Orders were given quickly to assemble at the North entrance, but witnesses said that it appeared that the police officers often faced as much chaos from their disordered ranks as they did from the protesters.

There is much more to be said from these two Appendices, but suffice it to say that fear of too dramatic intervention from the National Guard, coupled with lack of good coordination among the participating police forces, led to an ill-preparedness and the sad, sad sight of protesters disrupting the crucial session of Congress that would certify the winner of the 2020 Presidential election. In the end, Congress was recessed for about seven hours, but they doggedly returned to their work in the evening of January 6, and finally completed their work after 3:30 a.m. on the morning of January 7, 2021. The election of a new President-elect, Joe Biden, was finally certified, and the great experiment in representative democracy, bruised but still breathing, continued.

Questions for Discussion and Further Investigation

1. I argued above that one of the major reasons for slow deployment of the DC National Guard was fear. What was my thesis? Do you agree or disagree or want to develop the idea in any way?

2. What levels of authority or violence to ward off protesters do you believe these police forces should have had on January 6, 2021? Persuasion by words? Shoot to kill? Batons and clubs only?

3. I mentioned that three police forces, the US Capitol Police, the Metropolitan District of Columbia Police, and the United

States Park Police, had different but complementary jurisdiction on January 6, 2021. Explain their different roles.

4. When Congress re-convened at about 9:00 p.m. on January 6, it first had to deal with objections to the electoral vote from Arizona. Why was that? How was that handled?

CHAPTER 13

So What Do We Call What Happened on January 6, 2021?

Introduction

In this chapter I try to answer the question of what precisely we should call this "event" or "series of events" at the US Capitol beginning early in the afternoon and concluding early in the evening of January 6, 2021. The unprecedented events of that day allow for all kinds of rhetorical excess, as well as rhetorical minimization. An example of the latter is when one US Representative saw some of the protesters inside the Capitol as they were taking pictures of the figures in Statuary Hall; he said that if one looked only at a video of those activities they would appear no different than "tourists." Also, in attempting to minimize any blame of the protesters, one US Senator said that these people truly loved their country.

But then there were some Republicans, including Senate Majority leader Mitch McConnell, as well as many Democrats, who characterized the event as a "failed insurrection." The words describing the event were thrown around as if they themselves were grenades that might explode upon impact. Was it the "riot" of a "surging mob?" Or, perhaps an "insurrection?" Did the protesters "storm" the Capitol? Was it a "siege?" Were the protesters "rioters" or "terrorists" or "armed insurrectionists?" The January 6 Select Committee called it an "attack" on the US Capitol. Is that a helpful or true characterization? Or was the entry into the Capitol a "rebellion" or "insurgency" or "intrusion" or "incursion" or an "act of treason" which "attempted to lead an armed revolt against the United States government?" Were the protesters "rebels" or was it an attempt at a "violent takeover" or "violent disruption" of the United States government? Characterizations, like the evil spirits exiting the Gadarene demoniac at Jesus' command, are Legion.

My Approach

My approach to this difficult but fundamental question is to propose a rather minimalist definition that could be greatly expanded based on the conduct of any particular individual. That is, I try to come up with a definition that will account for the fact of great diversity among the protesters. That some might have said, "1776 All over Again!" or "Storm the Bastille!" doesn't make them all equally guilty of seditious conspiracy or treason.

My minimalist definition is this: January 6, 2021 witnessed an *illegal and terrifying occupation of the United States Capitol by a crowd which wanted to stop the lawful functioning of the Congress to declare Joe Biden President of the United States.* Let's look especially at a) illegal; b) terrifying and c) occupation.

First, I start with the concept of illegality because that is the hook our culture uses to assess blame in situations like this. In a word, several thousand people, almost a thousand of whom have now been identified and arrested by federal officials, broke the law and should pay the consequences duly written in the statute books for legal violations. Though it is beyond the scope of this essay to detail all the crimes, one can conveniently divide them into three categories: i) Crimes against Property; ii) Crimes relating to Disorder; and iii) More serious Crimes against the Government and the functioning of the United States Government.

We begin with an observation that any who broke down the fenced barriers to the Capitol or entered the grounds and then the Capitol were guilty of Trespass. Many people damaged federal property, either intentionally or unintentionally. Several federal statutes speak directly to crimes called "depredation against any property of the United States" (e.g., 18 USC 1361). The Architect of the Capitol is now estimating the damage of that day as upwards of $30 million. The protesters caused it. They should, to the best of our ability to hold people accountable, pay for it, either in fiscal assessments or jail time.

ii) There were Crimes related to Disorder. These included both attempts to impede or disrupt the functioning of government (cf. 18 USC Sec 1792) and attempts to obstruct or hurt federal law enforcement officers. More than 130 police were injured. Those who injured them committed criminal offenses. iii) The most serious Crimes related to attempts to stymie or even Conspire to Act Treasonously or Seditiously against the United States. A whole series of statues in 18 USC 2381ff and 115 USC 2383-2385 define these crimes more closely. In a word, as some commentators have said, there is an "avalanche" of criminal statutes implicated by the activity of protesters that should be used to hold people accountable.

Second, it was a *terrifying* as well as an illegal occupation. It was *terrifying* to the brave officers who tried to defend the bastion of our Democracy; it was *terrifying* to the Congressional staff and Members of Congress who had to huddle in rooms for many minutes until they could be hustled off to safety. It was *terrifying* for the American people who watched it via television—to see how the orderly functioning of government on this important day was impeded by the illegal occupation of the Capitol. We ought never to forget the *terror* of the day, because those doing the illegal activities, despite the difference in motivation, could simply not be trusted *not* to hurt or even kill people if they had the opportunity. When that kind of fear is injected into the heart of the central institutions of Democracy, people who are in the vicinity need to be held accountable.

Finally, it was, in my language, an *occupation*. I think that the language of *assault, attack, siege, storming,* as if the Capitol were some kind of latter-day Bastille, is not helpful language. Some of the protesters, to be sure, wanted to storm and threaten and even do violence if they had the opportunity. But the most neutral term, I think, is that the space was occupied—illegally of course—for several hours. We saw some of the occupiers, for example, using flags as weapons, breaking through windows, skewering officers, brandishing them threateningly. But others of the occupiers seemed to be more intent on getting some good video footage to show that they were in the Capitol. Some, of course brazenly took over the Speaker's office—but it was all with the goal, shared uniformly, of "stopping the steal" or stopping the legitimate functioning of the United States Congress.

Conclusion

Thus, I repeat, the events of that fateful afternoon on January 6, 2021 can best be characterized as an *illegal and terrifying occupation* of the United States Capitol—to prevent the certification of the 2020 Presidential election.

Questions for Discussion and Further Investigation

1. I have tried my best to define what happened on January 6, 2021 at the US Capitol. As you have studied this material,

watched videos, discussed it with others, and thought about it more deeply, how would you characterize that day? Would you use language like "attack" or "assault" or "insurrection" or "mob riot" or "tourist visit" or "occupation"?

2. What images are strongest in your mind, either from testimony you read or videos you saw, of events of that day in the US Capitol?

3. Many of the protesters have now been arrested and had trials, with the two garnering most news coverage being the trials of Stewart Rhodes and Kelly Meggs. Read about their trials, or the trials of others who were arrested, and report on what happened in at least one case.

4. Some of the protesters arrested were very young, even 18 or younger. Should special mercy or consideration be shown for younger protesters?

Appendix

Criminal Charges Recommended: What the Committee Couldn't Do

The purpose of this Appendix is to review briefly the criminal charges against President Donald Trump that the Committee feels are appropriate to be referred to the Special Prosecutor, Mr. Jack Smith (presented in pp. 103-113 of the Report). In addition, I review the types of information the committee *couldn't* get, largely because of opposition of many people to its work, opposition that resulted in many who may have actively refused to cooperate in giving testimony or even ignored Committee subpoenas.

The Charges against Donald Trump

As the Committee neared the end of its Executive Summary, the facts leading up to and taking place on January 6, 2021 were increasingly presented to fit the language of various federal criminal statutes so that the Special Prosecutor overseeing whether to charge former President Trump criminally would understand how Trump's behavior in planning for January 6 and summoning people to Washington DC that day could be understood as criminal behavior. The Committee selected five statutes which they felt Trump's behavior arguably violated.

First, his planning to disrupt the January 6 certification of Joe Biden's win arguably "corruptly obstructed, influenced or impeded an official proceeding" (18 USC sec 1512c).

Second, his various machinations with Prof Eastman and senior staff appeared to the Committee to have been a "conspiracy to defraud the United States" (18 USC sec 371).

Third, his submission of false slates of electors to Congress and the National Archives indicated to the Committee he had entered into a "conspiracy to make a false statement" (18 USC secs 371, 1001).

Fourth, his conduct leading up to and on January 6 indicated he had violated the law against "inciting" or "assisting" or "aiding and comforting" an insurrection (18 USC sec 2383).

Finally, the Committee felt like his behavior may have violated assorted other conspiracy statutes, such as 18 USC secs 372 and 2384. The point is that by building a case and presenting it in the Executive Summary, the Committee provides the next level of officials, especially Special Prosecutor Smith, a road map if he recommends bringing criminal charges against former President Trump.

It is beyond the scope of this essay to opine whether those charges will be filed, whether a trial happens and what the outcome will be. I think no one is in a position at this date (early 2023) to make anything more than conjectures on the subject.

What The Committee *Couldn't* Do

The first reaction of many readers of this most voluminous report might be that everything that could have been collected about the events leading up to and on the day of January 6, 2021 *must* have appeared in the Report. But that is far from the case. What this final section addresses is the committee's struggle for credibility as well as the kind of information, very valuable information, that is still "out there" and which the committee couldn't access. It might be helpful to summarize this in several observations.

First, the very composition of the committee may lead people to try to cast aspersions on its validity, objectivity or helpfulness. Of the nine members, only two were Republicans. The Committee helpfully presents the exchanges between Speaker Pelosi and Minority Leader McCarthy leading up to the appointment of the members (early Spring 2021), to show how the original plan, to have a committee of 5 Republicans and 5 Democrats quickly unraveled. Does that skew the results of the Committee? Perhaps, but not as much as one might think. Why? Well. . . .

Second, in order to deal with the issue of potential bias, the Committee decided that almost all their witnesses (that would be about five dozen witnesses) would be Republicans. That is, the evidence gathered would not only be from those in the know, but those who were committed to the President before the events of January 6, 2021. Several of the witnesses gave crucial testimony, testimony that both brought the Committee inside the strategizing and conflict in the White House between November 3, 2020 and January 6, 2021 and showed that the major pre-occupation of the President in those days was to deny he had lost the election and to seek any means possible to overturn the election results.

Third, the Committee is aware that many people "in the know" either refused to testify or repeatedly "took the Fifth" when testifying, as a clear strategy of obfuscating or trying to deny vital information to the Committee. The Committee recommends that the House Ethics Committee look into the potential ethical violations of members who refused to acknowledge Committee subpoenas. With the Republicans gaining a majority in the House in the 2022 Congressional elections, there seems little chance that this request will go anywhere.

Fourth, the Committee became aware of discussions of broad pardons for many architects of aspects of the plan to keep President Trump in power by whatever means they could. To the Committee this action smacks of legal liability. But the Committee felt stymied as they tried to peel back the layers of discussions swirling around potential pardons.

Fifth, the Committee realizes that many actors outside of the Committee have or will be developing valuable information relating to its charge. One such prominent instance is the case of Prof John Eastman in a CA Federal District Court, where Judge Carter issued rulings that may make available many of Eastman's emails that he argued were covered by attorney-client privilege. One can expect other cases across the country to yield helpful information.

We can expect additional information to continue to dribble out in the future. For example, we now know the Report was referring to Cassidy Hutchinson, rather than an anonymous witness, when it said her "Trump world" lawyer seemed more interested in defending the "boss" than in providing effective representation for her.

Questions for Discussion and Further Investigation

1. Some have suggested that referring criminal charges against a former President to a special prosecutor is dangerous business for a democracy, since it risks turning the political process into a criminal process for those who have lost. Do you agree with that statement?
2. Look at the list of witnesses (page 131) whom the Committee called to testify before it. Select one or two and see what you can find out about them and their testimony.
3. I listed several federal statutes that the Committee says that

President Trump likely violated. Find those statutes in the United States Code, read them, and try to understand what they mean.

4. An important case against Professor Eastman is *John C. Eastman v Bennie G. Thompson et al.*, in the Central District of California (Federal Court). Find information about that case and try to figure out what happened there.

5. The Committee said it plans to send the criminal charges against President Trump to the Special Prosecutor. Who is that and what does he do?

Made in the USA
Monee, IL
20 March 2023

30223697R00059